DATE DUE

DEMCO 38-297

THE NEZ PERCE

MADELYN KLEIN ANDERSON

THE NEZ PERCE

Franklin Watts   *New York*   *Chicago*   *London*   *Toronto*   *Sydney*   *A First Book*

Map by Joe LeMonnier
Cover photograph copyright ©: Finders/Field Museum/R. Flanagan

Photographs copyright ©: Ben Klaffke: p. 3; North Wind Picture Archives,
Alfred, Me.: pp. 13, 17, 26, 28, 30, 39, 45, 47, 57; Allen Slickpoo, Sr.: p.
14; University of Washington, Special Collections, photo by Latham,
(#4920): p. 19; Idaho Historical Society: pp. 23, 35, 41, 50; Stock
Montage/Historical Pictures Service, Chicago, Il.: pp. 53, 55; Smithsonian
Institution, Washington, D.C.: p. 59; Franco Marinai/Sandra Orter:.p. 64

Library of Congress Cataloging-in-Publication Data

Anderson, Madelyn Klein.
The Nez Perce / by Madelyn Klein Anderson.
p. cm. — (A First book)
Includes bibliographical references and index.
ISBN 0-531-20063-9 — ISBN 0-531-15686-9 (pbk.)
1. Nez Perce Indians—History—Juvenile literature. 2. Nez Perce
Indians—Social life and customs—Juvenile literature. [1. Nez Perce
Indians. 2. Indians of North America.] I. Title.
II. Series.
E99.N5A55   1994
973'.04974—dc20   93-31422 CIP AC

CONTENTS

113 6206

BLOOD OF
THE MONSTER

In the beginning, a giant monster roamed the land, killing everything in its path. Word of this reached Coyote, that most clever of animals, who set out to destroy the monster before it ate the world. Coyote followed its trail of destruction and soon came face-to-face with the creature. "Ah!" roared the monster when it saw Coyote, and its mouth opened wide in a smile of pleasure at the thought of the feast to come. But clever Coyote quickly catapulted between the beast's teeth and down its throat, until he reached its heart. Then he stabbed and stabbed again with the flint blade he carried in his mouth until the monster fell dead. Coyote cut his way out of the body, flinging pieces about as he went. Being very clever, Coyote turned the pieces of monster into people. These people he sent to live in the forests or the mountains or on the plains, depending on the part of the monster from which they were made. When he was all done, or so he thought, Coyote realized that he had not put any people in the best place of all, the beautiful valley of Kamiah. So he squeezed out a few drops of blood from the heart of the monster and turned them into the best people of all, the Real People.

The Real People — in their Sahaptin language, the *Nimpau* — told this story for thousands of years, for so long that they forgot how they had really come to the Kamiah Valley. Yet that, too, was an amazing story: they walked across the ocean floor from Asia about 12,000 years ago.

It was a time of great cold, an ice age, and the ocean froze. Because frozen water shrinks in volume, the ocean waters shrank and pulled back from the land. Where Asia is closest to North America, at what we call the Bering Strait, the ocean floor was uncovered. This floor acted as a path or bridge between the two continents. The bridge appeared three times over the centuries, in three ice ages, and each time hunters and their families crossed it as they searched for game. Over many centuries, these great migrations of Asian peoples fanned out across North, South, and Central America, and today we know them as "Indians" and "Eskimos."

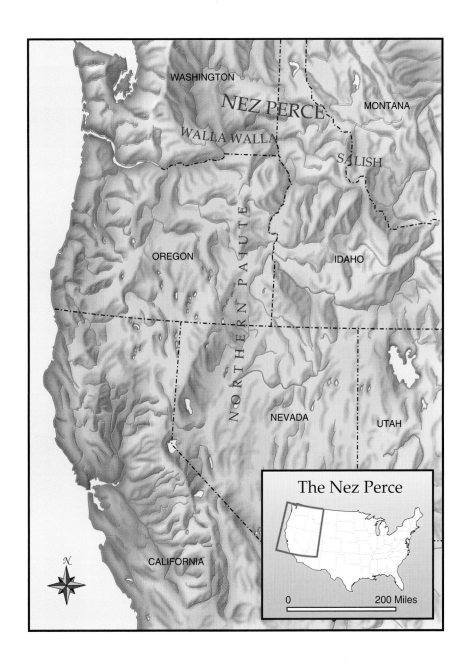

The Nez Perce

0   200 Miles

The Nimpau probably were among the last to arrive. They were part of a family known today as *Penutians*, along with the Cayuse, Klamath, Umatilla, WallaWalla, Appaloosa, and Klikitat groups who settled not far south of the bridge. About 10,000 years ago, members of the family moved eastward along the valley of the great Columbia River until they found the high plateau country between the two mountain ranges we now call the Cascades and the Rockies. It was a land of many rivers, of high meadows and deep canyons, a land that isolated and protected and fed them. And here they stayed.

The Nimpau spread out along the banks of the rivers — the Columbia and the Clearwater, the Salmon and the Snake — and the dozens of small streams that fed the rivers. They broke into settlements, so that they would not strip the rivers of fish or the land of game. The members of each settlement lived together in one large, circular house with the floor dug below ground level and with flat roofs of earth or mats made of grasses and reeds. As families grew, the houses were made bigger. Within the house each family had its own space and cooking fire; openings in the roof let out the smoke. A mound-shaped sweat house was always nearby for the men to cleanse themselves physically and mentally by sitting around a pile of heated stones and sweating from every pore until they were dizzy.

THE DALLES OF THE COLUMBIA RIVER, WHERE A NUMBER OF
WATERWAYS CONNECT — AN IMPORTANT TRADING PLACE TO
WHICH MEN TRAVELED FROM HUNDREDS OF MILES AWAY.

THIS LATE NINETEENTH-CENTURY PHOTO SHOWS A GROUP OF NEZ PERCE
CHIEFS ON HORSEBACK. THE NEZ PERCE HAD NO SINGLE CHIEF BUT
RATHER MANY CHIEFS WHO WERE RESPONSIBLE FOR ASPECTS OF TRIBAL
LIFE. NOTE THE FEATHERS WORN BY THE CHIEFS, WHICH WERE A LATER
ADDITION TO NEZ PERCE APPAREL ACQUIRED FROM THE PLAINS INDIANS.

The women probably did not use the sweat houses but kept themselves clean in other ways, for they were noted among other groups for their cleanliness — and their modesty. They covered their bodies with a one-piece soft leather dress that reached to the ankles, decorated with porcupine quills and seashells brought to them by travelers from the coast.

The Nimpau men often did not dress at all but decorated themselves with paints. Sometimes they wore a *breechclout* for protection. In the winter, they added capes of shredded bark or robes of elk skin with soft neck pieces of brown otter skin and braided grass, leg wrappings, and basketry hats. The favored hairstyle for both men and women was two braids hanging over the chest. A kind of pompadour, or roll of hair above the forehead, became popular with the men, who adorned these hairdos with shells and feathers.

The men who made ten *coups* during a raid were called chiefs. Chiefs might become important in their group, but no chief had any right to tell other Nimpau what to do unless they decided they needed such guidance for a particular reason. The people might agree on a leader in time of war, but he would not be alone in planning the war. He would have to meet with a chief of horses, a chief of hunting, a chief of camps, and other chiefs. And the warriors would have to decide whether the chiefs' plans pleased them, or they wouldn't go to war. In times of peace, if a council was called for any reason, it was attended only by those who agreed with what was going to be discussed. No one told anyone to do anything. A suggestion might be made: "It might be good to go hunting today." Those who wanted to hunt that day went hunting, those who didn't might go instead the following day or whenever. If things were not going the way some of them liked over a period of time, they simply moved upstream or down and set up another fishing settlement.

Men hunted and fished, and women gathered roots for food. When they became too old to do this, they became teachers. Both men and women could become *shamans*. Shamans were spiritual guides and treated the sick — a dangerous occupation, because the relatives of a patient who died were free to kill the doctor. Those who felt they had the power or who felt they had been chosen to become a shaman took the chance, however. This personal conviction might have come from childhood.

At some time between the ages of nine and fifteen, girls and boys went from the settlement to some personal place to wait for a revelation of a personal spirit, a *wyakin,* their guide and guardian through life. Without food, water, or sleep, the semiconscious

AN ARTIST'S IDEA OF HOW THE INDIANS FISHED. NETTING
WAS PROBABLY ONLY USED FOR SALMON FISHING WHEN
THEY WERE IN SEASON. THE NEZ PERCE ALSO CAUGHT
FISH IN TRAPS, OR WEIRS.

child might well experience something he or she felt was the revelation of a spirit guardian. The child alone interpreted the meaning of the experience and could never tell anyone about it. Sometimes, at the Guardian Spirit Dance in the depth of winter, a hint might be dropped, but never more than that. Not everyone found a spirit guardian. Some children became too frightened or too hungry or impatient, but they did not pretend to have found a spirit, for that would bring misfortune. They or their families might get hurt or suffer from hunger in the dark, cold days of winter.

Hunting and fishing did not yield much food in winter, and then the people ate a kind of mush made from roasting the inner fibers of tree bark. They also had a supply of dried cakes made from a root called *kouse* (pronounced koo-see). Kouse was gathered in the spring and cooked and shaped into a kind of patty and sun-dried for storage, but only after the Nimpau had their fill of delicious fresh-boiled kouse.

In the summer, the Nimpau walked for miles to meadows carpeted with blue-flowered *camas*, wild lilies with bulbous roots that look like small onions but taste sweet. They pitched their summer *tepees* of skins, and while the women and girls dug out the cama bulbs with their curved sticks, the men gambled and played games or hunted.

THIS PHOTO FROM THE EARLY 1900S SHOWS THE NEZ PERCE
CELEBRATING THE CAMAS FESTIVAL WITH MANY WHITES LOOKING
ON. UNFORTUNATELY, TRADITIONAL INDIAN CELEBRATIONS AND
FESTIVALS BECAME TOURIST ATTRACTIONS FOR EASTERNERS.

The hunters used bows made from wood or the great curled horns of mountain sheep. About 3 feet (1 m) long, they were backed by deer *sinew* attached with a glue made from scraped salmon skin or boiled sturgeon. Hunters left the settlements for months at a time, breaking new trails to reach more game. They also reached other people, who greatly admired their bows and arrows. It was not long before the men realized that they could get much more than game with their bows, and they became traders as well as hunters. The world of the Nimpau was growing beyond the Kamiah Valley where Coyote had put them.

INTO THE WORLD

When horses entered their lives, in the early 1700s, the Nimpau could journey still farther from their homeland. They could trade for more goods. They could learn from other people things that could make them more powerful. The horse gave them these riches.

The horse had once lived on the North American continent but had become extinct. Then the Spanish explorers brought their Arabian horses to America in the 1500s. Indians who rebelled against Spanish rule set free hundreds of these horses, and the West soon filled with wild herds that numbered in the many thousands.

A NEZ PERCE IN HIS NEW-STYLE CLOTHING AND MOUNTED
ON ONE OF HIS ALL-IMPORTANT HORSES.

It is said that the Cayuse introduced the Nimpau, their neighbors and relatives, to the horse. The Cayuse have been credited with everything connected to horses — western ponies even became known as cayuses. Actually, the Nimpau were probably the greater horsemen. Though untaught, they devised breeding techniques that produced horses with ideal qualities of strength, speed, and endurance. The Appaloosas, other Nimpau relatives, gave their name to a famed breed of horses with spotted rumps, but it was the Nimpau who bred them.

Every Nimpau family had their own herd of horses, often a very large herd numbering in the hundreds. Their horses carried the Nimpau and their trade goods across the Rocky Mountains to the Great Plains. Now they could bring with them not only more bows but also large amounts of dried fish and salmon oil packed in fish skins. And they could bring home the skins and meat of the buffalo and the feathered bonnets, beads, and pipes of the Plains Indians, particularly the Crow. The men even adopted the dress of the Crow — skin leggings and a shirt, certainly more practical than a breechclout for long journeys astride a horse. But when they were decorated with beautiful Crow beadwork, those outfits got so heavy that they could hardly be considered practical. They were impressive, however, and that is the way they were used, to impress friends and foes at formal gatherings.

Not only did their lifestyle change, but even the Nimpau name changed. Other groups had long called them the Blue or the Green or the Brown People, depending on their name for the land of the Nimpau. But it was now that the Shoshoni people came to call them the Cho-Pun-Osh, or Pierced Noses, and no one really knows why that was. Wearing a ring or a tubular dentalium shell in the nose was common among the Northwest Coast Indians who were related to the Nimpau, and it might have been a Nimpau custom in ancient times. Or the Shoshoni might have confused them with their relatives. Whatever the reason, Cho-Pun-Osh they were — in sign language, a finger at the nostril.

When the Shoshonis told French Canadian fur trappers of the Cho-Pun-Osh on the other side of the Rockies, the trappers translated the name into their own words for pierced noses, "Nez Percé," pronounced "Nay Pair-say." This was later Americanized into "Nezz Purse." And the Nimpau answered to the name and became known in written history as the Nez Perce.

Other changes were less acceptable to the Nimpau, or Nez Perce. Coyote's land grant to the Nimpau did not mean much to neighboring

Spokanes, Coeur d'Alenes, Snakes (the western Shoshonis, northern Paiutes, and the Bannocks), and particularly the Blackfeet. And when the nomadic Cheyennes, Arapahoes, Utes, Kiowas, and Comanches got word of the Nez Perce raids for horses and slaves, particularly women slaves, became common. Most raids meant a raid in revenge.

Raids were usually little more than small forays under the cover of darkness to retrieve or replace the horses (not the women) that had been stolen. There were some, however, that were full battles. For these, the warriors decorated themselves and their horses with war paint made from colored powders mixed with grease. They painted their forehead and the center part in their feather-decorated hair a bright red or orange. On their eyelids, cheeks, and bodies they painted dots or dashes of yellow, red, green, or black, usually in a pattern that represented their guardian spirit. Their horses were as colorful: heads and necks yellow and red, manes black, and bodies a symbolic mix of stripes, circles, and zigzags. The tails were painted red and tied with ribbons that fanned out in a brilliant display as they galloped into battle.

Warriors were often joined by the women. The women did not actually fight, but they added numbers and noise to the attack. They cheered their men on and screamed insults at the enemy. They stood

OLD ENGRAVING OF AN INDIAN RAID AS
IMAGINED BY THE ARTIST

watch over the wounded and dead and brought up fresh horses when they were needed. When the fighting was victorious, the women danced around their prisoners and tormented them. A favored practice was to force them to hold up the scalps of their dead family members and friends. But prisoners were usually not harmed physically, because they had to serve as slaves.

A Nez Perce woman who was taken prisoner in a raid by Canadian Indians, probably the Cree, was the first of her people to see a white man. He bought her from her captors, married her, and brought her to a white settlement to live. She liked the white people and was grateful for their medicine that helped the eye disease, *trachoma*, that she, like many other Nez Perce, suffered from. But when she had a child she wanted to go back to her homeland. After months of wandering, during which her baby died, she was found by a party of Salish hunters, who brought her to her people. It was her fond recollection of the whites that led her to ask her people to welcome the white men of the Lewis and Clark expedition rather than kill them.

Meriwether Lewis and William Clark headed a group of explorers who were working their way across the North American continent, mapping the country and searching for inhabitants. They came upon the

MERIWETHER LEWIS (LEFT)
AND WILLIAM CLARK (RIGHT)

Nez Perce in 1805. They called them by their Shoshoni name, Cho-Pun-Osh, and told of seeing two or three men with pierced noses — whether they were Nimpau or visitors cannot be known. This is the only recorded sighting of the Nez Perce with pierced noses.

Lewis and Clark were very favorably impressed by the intelligence, honesty, and good fellowship of the Nez Perce. Although Nez Perce land did not at the time belong to either the United States or Canada, Lewis and Clark knew that one day it would, and they wanted it for their country. It must have been impossible for the Indians — who had never even heard the name "Indians" before — to understand what the white men meant when they spoke of belonging to a great country with a great white father who promised to watch over them. They listened politely but paid no mind to the words that meant nothing. The Earth that was their Mother did not belong to anyone. And if this person who called himself the Great White Father wanted to lead them, that did not mean they would follow. They had never done anything they did not want to do. That was the Nimpau way.

So they listened to the white men without concern. They liked Lewis and Clark and their men very

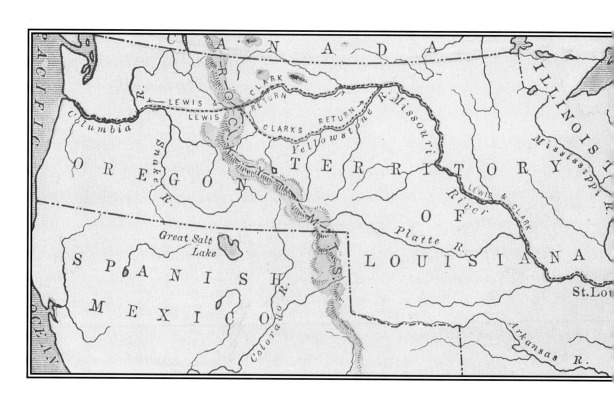

ROUTE TAKEN BY THE LEWIS AND CLARK EXPEDITION TO
EXPLORE THE NEWLY ACQUIRED LOUISIANA TERRITORY
AND LAY CLAIM TO THE OREGON TERRITORY

much. They admired their words, their wisdom, their tools, their compasses, their books.

Over the years that followed, they talked about them with much pleasure. They reasoned that these white men had to have a special way to reach the very powerful gods that gave them so many wondrous things. The key, they thought, lay in the magic in the white men's books. And years later they did something very remarkable to get these magical writings for themselves.

WHITE MAGIC

French, English, and then American fur trappers soon followed the path of Lewis and Clark. A British trading post was set up by the Hudson's Bay Company in Nez Perce territory. It was followed by a military post, first called "Fort Nez Perce," then "Fort Walla Walla."

The Nez Perce got guns and whiskey, but neither seemed to be a big problem to them. The guns helped them defend themselves against their old enemies, made hunting easier, and kept them on an equal relationship with others when they went buffalo hunting. The buffalo themselves were not usually killed by guns but by being herded and driven over steep cliffs to die in the canyon below. As for whiskey, the Nez Perce were too intelligent to allow themselves to be befuddled by alcohol, at least not often, and then only occasionally among the young men.

Relationships between the Nez Perce and the newcomers were peaceful, and many of the trappers built houses and settled down with Nez Perce wives and raised families. Stories were told around campfires of Lewis and Clark and the great cities and many people to the east. The Nez Perce could not envision any harm from these people and spoke only of the magic they might learn from them. Finally, a council of chiefs decided to send men to St. Louis, where their old friend William Clark was the Superintendent for Indian affairs, to bring back books and teachers.

Three Nez Perce reached St. Louis safely in 1831 and were warmly welcomed by Clark. They made a strong impression on the whites and were much admired, but the extraordinary venture seemed to end with no result. It was not until five years later that a Protestant church group decided to finance the work of a missionary to convert the Nez Perce to Christianity and to teach them the white ways they mistakenly thought the Indians were seeking. The Nez Perce were very happy with their own ways and wanted only the white men's magic, their power.

Instead they got the very opposite of what they sought. They learned to read but lost their power to decide for themselves how they wanted to live.

The Presbyterian missionaries were Dr. Marcus Whitman and his wife, Narcissa, and Henry Spalding and his new bride, Eliza. Whitman, the head of the group, concentrated on the Cayuse. The Spaldings built a mission in the valley of Lapwai, a location that reminded them of their home in the farmland of upstate New York, and took on the Nez Perce.

The missionaries worked hard to turn the Nez Perce from hunters and gatherers into farmers. They felt strongly that the Indians' only chance for survival as the country inevitably filled up with settlers was to live like them, to work and dress like them, and to follow the Christian religion. Spalding forbade the Nez Perce to go buffalo hunting, for this took the men away from their Christian studies and their jobs of cultivating farmland. He forbade tribal dances and the gambling the Nez Perce enjoyed. This was a heavy price for the Nez Perce to pay, too heavy for some. Digging and raking and plowing meant inflicting great indignity and pain on the Earth, their Mother. And while it meant better supplies of food in the winter, it meant a lot less pleasure at other times. Worse, the Nez Perce had to accept a system

EARLY MISSIONARIES ATTEMPTED TO ENCOURAGE THE NEZ PERCE
TO BECOME FARMERS. BY THE TIME OF THE 1889 PRESIDENTIAL ORDER
TO BREAK UP THE TRIBE, MANY NEZ PERCE LIVED BY FARMING. ALICE
FLETCHER OF HARVARD UNIVERSITY AND A SPECIALIST IN INDIAN
AFFAIRS MADE A CAREFUL SURVEY OF ALL NEZ PERCE TO ENSURE
THAT ALL ENTITLED SHARED IN RESERVATION LANDS.

of harsh discipline that violated their pride and independence.

Spalding meant well but was anxious to show results to the mission board at home. He reasoned that these people had to be taught by a very strict father. He himself had never known a father — his mother was unmarried — and perhaps that is why his punishments were not fatherly and involved a great deal of whipping. He had one Nez Perce woman given seventy lashes for leaving the white husband who beat her. This made little sense to the Nez Perce, who felt that the husband deserved the punishment.

Spalding's almost maniacal temper added to the unhappiness of several new missionaries who were sent to Lapwai. They wrote long letters of complaint to the mission board, until Spalding was dismissed. Dr. Whitman went back east to get the board to rescind its order. In his absence, Dr. Elijah White showed up. White, a missionary from another area and the United States subagent for Indian affairs in Oregon, brought a written code of punishments to help Spalding maintain order among the Nez Perce.

The wonder is that any of the proud, intelligent Nez Perce would accept such a code, but accept it they did. They themselves inserted the ninth pro-

The Missionary's Code for the Nez Perce

1. Whoever wilfully takes life shall be hung.

2. Whoever burns a dwelling house shall be hung.

3. Whoever burns an outbuilding shall be imprisoned six months, receive 50 lashes, and pay all damages.

4. Whoever carelessly burns a house or any property shall pay damages.

5. If anyone enter a dwelling, without permission of the occupant, the chiefs shall punish him as they think proper.

6. If anyone steal, he shall pay back two fold, and if it be the value of a beaver skin or less, he shall receive 25 lashes and if the value is over a beaver skin he shall pay back two fold and receive 50 lashes.

7. If anyone take a horse, and ride it without permission, or take any article and use it without liberty, he shall pay for the use of it, and receive from 20 to 50 lashes as the chief shall direct.

8. If anyone enter a field and injure the crops, or throw down the fence, so that cattle and horses shall go in and do damage, he shall pay all the damages and receive 25 lashes for every offense.

9. Those only may keep dogs who travel or live among the game. If a dog kill a lamb, calf, or any domestic animal, the owner shall pay the damages and kill the dog.

10. If an Indian raise a gun or other weapon against a white man, it shall be reported to the chiefs and they shall punish him. If a white person do the same to an Indian, it shall be reported to Dr. White and he shall redress it.

11. If an Indian break these laws, he shall be punished by his chief. If a white man break them, he shall be reported to the agent and be punished at his instance.

vision. That is, the farmers among them did. Others ignored the code. After all, they had not agreed to it and did not consider themselves bound by it. They soon learned that this did not matter to the white men, who believed in majority rule. Dr. White, as Indian agent, insisted that the Nez Perce select someone to act as head chief to speak and be responsible for the actions of the whole tribe. This they did, but many moved away, to where they could be free of missionaries. And so it came to pass that the Nez Perce were divided into two nations, the upper or mission Nez Perce and the lower non-mission Nez Perce.

The mission Nez Perce fared much better with Eliza Spalding than with the male missionaries. She could calm tempers and gain cooperation through reason rather than beatings. She also gave the Nez Perce what they wanted: the ability to read and write. Mrs. Spalding was a remarkable young woman who worked hard to benefit the Indians. She reasoned that it would be easier for the Nez Perce to learn to read and write in the language they spoke, Sahaptin, than in English. So she learned to speak Sahaptin and then devised an alphabet based on its sounds. Her students — some two hundred of them — eagerly copied the works she wrote down for them

LAPWAI

in the new alphabet. They took the copies home to teach others. When the Hawaiian missions donated a small printing press to their fellow missionaries at Lapwai, Eliza Spalding translated and supervised the printing of about a dozen books into Sahaptin. The Nez Perce greatly respected — even loved — their caring, gentle teacher and the child she bore.

The mission Nez Perce learned enough farming to keep from starving in winter. They grew corn and other vegetables and raised some cattle. They learned what the missionaries knew of curing illness, which was really little more than the shamans already knew. When Spalding taught himself the art of *bloodletting*, a favorite cure-all of the times, the Nez Perce happily learned to cut into veins, too — sometimes to the point of dying from infection or loss of blood.

Although the Nez Perce were grateful for the things they were taught, they wanted more than the religious texts the Spaldings gave them. This they did not get. When the missionaries suggested that their sons be sent east to school, a few families made the sacrifice so that their sons might gain the knowledge the group lacked. But when the few young men who survived the illnesses and dangers of the cities returned in their white men's clothing and with white men's ways, there was little place for them. Their

SCHOOLGIRLS WERE MADE TO DRESS IN
EUROPEAN-STYLE CLOTHES BUT THEY PLAYED
WITH THEIR OWN TOYS.

education did not help their people in any concrete way, and certainly their own identities were confused. Some went back to tribal life, and a few returned to the cities.

And more and more people left the cities as word of the missionaries' work and peaceful Christian Indian farmers made prospective settlers feel safe. They came slowly at first and then in increasing numbers. Alarmed, the missionaries increased their efforts to make the Indians fit into the new society that would soon envelop them.

A BITTER END

On the whole, the Nez Perce were more civilized and better educated than many of the new settlers who looked down on them. But there seemed to be nothing they could do to protect their way of life or their lands against the invaders who were so sure of their superiority and right to rule.

Gradually, the Nez Perce sold land to the settlers. The Nez Perce were canny business people, and they extracted a good price for their lands. But when the settlers wanted more, some of them just took it. They argued that the Nez Perce had lots of land, and they did — some 44,000 square miles (70,840 sq km) covering what is now western Idaho, northeast Oregon, and southeast Washington. It is estimated that at the time there were somewhat more than 4,000 Nez Perce, so that was roughly 11 square miles (almost 18 sq km) for each man, woman, or child. They argued that the Nez Perce were not really farmers and did not cultivate the land to its full potential, and they did not. Even if they had wanted to, they really did not have the time, because Lapwai rules required them to attend church services twice daily. The fact that it was Nez Perce land to do with as they saw fit was something the newcomers simply did not see. They saw instead a promised land for themselves, with great rewards of riches and freedom for their children and their children's children. Generations who in Europe would never have had anything could achieve everything in this new land. So they flocked to these lands encouraged by the government who wanted to strengthen the United States' claim to the Oregon Territory. One of their main routes followed the Oregon Trail — an old Nez Perce trading trail part of the way.

Through it all, the Nez Perce held the peace. The nonmission Nez Perce voiced their anger in harmless ways. The young men dashed around on their horses, whooping and knocking over a few things just to put a good scare into the intruders. But Dr. White's code of punishments was being applied more frequently and less fairly. The Nez Perce honored their bargains and

AN OLD ENGRAVING — ALMOST A CARTOON — OF SETTLERS ON
THE OREGON TRAIL WITH NOT A WOMAN OR CHILD IN SIGHT
ALTHOUGH THEY WERE SURELY THERE.

carried out the punishments the code required, but whites were rarely punished for their misdoings. Discontent and resentment grew, until, in December 1847, it erupted in a murderous rage. A band of drunken young men decided to rid themselves of these invaders. The men may possibly have been Nez Perce, but it is more likely they were Cayuse. They were led by a Cayuse who was seeking to avenge his father's death at the hands of a white man who had gone unpunished. The group galloped about the countryside, seeking out the men who had been offensive to them, and they killed them. Then they killed Dr. and Mrs. Whitman and fourteen or fifteen white men and boys at the Whitman mission and kidnapped about forty women and children. They went on to Lapwai to find Henry Spalding. They found instead Eliza Spalding, who stood up to them in her husband's absence from home and asked for and received help from the older Nez Perce chiefs. At the same time, other Nez Perce were helping her husband to evade capture.

The Presbyterian presence among the Nez Perce was weakened for a long while after this. The Catholic missionaries in the north, who had never had as strong a hold on the Nez Perce, continued to go quietly about their work. Those Nez Perce who had enjoyed the Presbyterian rites continued to practice them.

AN ENGRAVING BY
FREDERIC REMINGTON OF
A CAYUSE AND HIS HORSE

They did not work on Sundays, they sang hymns, they read their Bibles, and they held church services as best they could. Newly arrived settlers, fearful of what they might face after the killings at the Whitman mission, were astounded — and relieved.

The Nez Perce were, of course, not the only Indians being invaded and treated like inferiors in their own lands. They were luckier than some, however, in that their population was not devastated by the new diseases unknowingly spread among the Indians by the settlers. In those days no one knew how to protect against communicable disease. Smallpox killed or scarred and tuberculosis and cholera ravaged whites and Indians alike. But simple childhood diseases such as measles caused many deaths among Indians.

The United States government decided to protect the Indians against all this devastation being brought to them. The government's plan was to set aside, or reserve, large areas of land called *reservations* for the sole use of the Indians. No others could own property there or hunt on it or use it in any way. This was to be guaranteed by treaty. While this was well meant, it also meant that the settlers would be guaranteed nonreservation lands that had belonged to the Indians. In 1850, the Donation Land Act granted families the right to 640 acres (259 ha) of western land — Indian land — free.

The Nez Perce were asked to sell about 4,000 square miles (6,480 sq km) of their land, leaving them with a still considerable amount reserved to themselves. They met in council to discuss the treaty being offered them, and soon split into two groups, treaty and nontreaty. At this point, many mission Nez Perce turned their backs on the missionaries and joined with the nontreaty group. No one knows how many Nez Perce were in each group, a point that was to become important when a later treaty was signed. But the treaty they were being offered was signed by more than fifty chiefs and went into effect in 1855. Problems soon arose.

As was their custom, those Nez Perce who did not agree to the treaty did not consider themselves bound by it. The government did not see it that way and assumed that they had a treaty with all the Nez Perce. When they realized they didn't, they offered the nontreaty Indians small homesteads. Unfortunately, these were often inside larger areas being acquired by settlers. When the settlers bought the Nez Perce out, they did so at a price that satisfied the Indians. But sometimes the settlers simply stole the lands and forced the Indians off. Other settlers were sure that the land reserved to the Nez Perce was better than theirs, and they wanted it. They also wanted to contain the Nez Perce on a smaller, more

JASON WAS SENT TO WASHINGTON, D.C., AS A
REPRESENTATIVE OF THE NEZ PERCE TO PROTEST
THE CONTINUED MOVEMENT OF SETTLERS AND
MINERS INTO NEZ PERCE LANDS.

manageable reservation to avoid uprisings similar to those taking place elsewhere. To add to the problem, a gold rush in 1860 brought in many prospectors who decided that the best place to make a strike was on reservation lands. This was a dangerous mix of conflicting ideas, and tensions grew.

The government sent representatives to the Nez Perce to change the treaty terms. They proposed a reservation of roughly one-fourth the size of the first, and far to the north of the areas favored by the Nez Perce.

Treaty and nontreaty Nez Perce alike were astonished that the Great White Father in Washington could break his word in this way. But still they did not go to war. The government negotiator rounded up enough signers to make it seem as if the majority of the Nez Perce had agreed to the treaty. Actually, the signers were only from the treaty Nez Perce, and they agreed to give up lands that belonged to the nontreaty group. And when the treaty was formalized in Washington, in 1863 the complicated boundaries got even more confused — whether accidentally or deliberately, it is not known — and the Nez Perce lost much of the desirable lands they thought were theirs forever. It was the last of 375 treaties negotiated by the U.S. government, and it was not one of which to be proud.

It was no wonder that a new all-Indian religion took hold of many Indians by now, including the Nez Perce. It was a simple religion, started by a Columbia River neighbor of the Nez Perce. He told of his dreams or visions of the whites being driven out of the land and the return of the Indians to their old ways. All the dead animals would come to life so that there would be plenty of food, and the Indian would not have to harm his Mother the Earth by plowing or planting. This Dreamer Religion, as it was known to the whites, was seen as a threat and it was banned but practiced secretly.

Perhaps the Nez Perce felt some of these dreams were coming true when an Executive Order was signed by President Ulysses S. Grant in 1873 reserving to the Nez Perce their beloved Wallowa, Grande Ronde, and Immaha valleys. But in 1875 the order was rescinded, and it was to the Wallowa Valley that the largest band of nontreaty Nez Perce was attached. Chief Joseph, who was to become one of the most famous Indians of all time, had buried his father, old Joseph, here. He had promised him as he lay dying that he would never leave the Wallowa Valley. Old Joseph had been another great chief of the Nez Perce and one of Spalding's first converts. He had turned from Christianity to the Dreamer Religion and, although he had signed the 1855 treaty, he had

CHIEF JOSEPH, WHOSE SAHAPTIN NAME WAS
HIN-MAH-TOO-YAH-LAT-KEKHUT

become a leader of the nontreaty Nez Perce. Now his sons were being asked to betray his teachings. They and all the others were being asked to leave the ancestral land, their dead, behind. The chiefs tried to negotiate, tried to make the government keep its promise to them.

But in June 1877, on the last day remaining for the nontreaty Nez Perce to move onto the reservation, a small band of drunken men took up arms against the whites and killed a number of them. The chiefs — Joseph and his brother Ollikut and Looking Glass and Toohoolhoolzote and White Bird and others — had run out of time. Now there could be no more negotiations.

The chiefs led the nontreaty Nez Perce away from their homeland. There were about four hundred of them, at least half of them women and children. At first they moved south and east. Perhaps they hoped to join another tribe, but if so, they found no welcome and no land safer or more free than the land they had left. So they turned north, making a huge U-loop, and headed for the Canadian border, where other of the Nez Perce had gone before them. Canada, like the United States, had a reservation system for Indians, but there were fewer settlers there and better hunting.

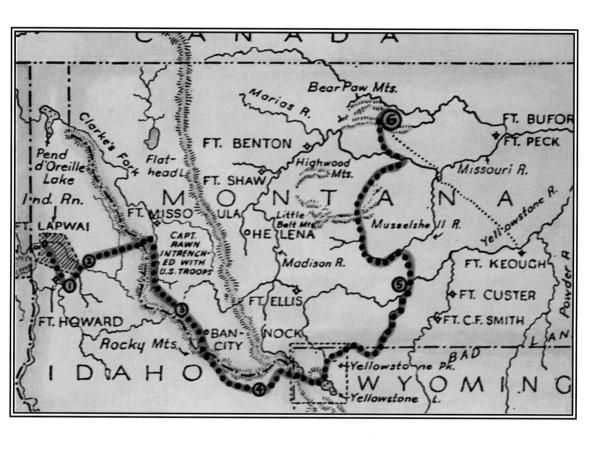

ROUTE OF THE FLEEING NEZ PERCE BAND

A large band of Indians on the move made the U.S. government and military uneasy. The settlers were fearful to the point of hysteria. General George Armstrong Custer and his men had been wiped out just the year before by the Sioux massing at Little Big Horn. Were the Nez Perce connecting up with other tribes for another armed rebellion? Were they going to kill settlers and destroy their property? They had to be moved onto the reservation. The cavalry was dispatched to bring them in.

The Nez Perce avoided the soldiers brilliantly. And when they could not avoid them, they fought. They used sophisticated tactics such as trench warfare that astounded their pursuers, among them old Indian fighters like Colonel (later General) Nelson Miles and General Oliver Howard. During this four-month-long trek of over 1,000 miles (1,600 km) through narrow canyons and across mountains and swift-flowing rivers, five major battles and many more small engagements took place. Men and women were killed — the women in the thick of battle supplying their men with fresh horses and reloading guns. Babies were born, children and old people died. And on the other side, as many or more soldiers and civilian volunteers were killed or wounded or struck down by disease.

MAJOR GENERAL O.O. HOWARD (LEFT) AND
MAJOR GENERAL NELSON A. MILES (RIGHT)

Among the Nez Perce dead were two great chiefs who had worked out the strategies to Looking Glass and Toohoolhoolzote, as well as Joseph's brother Ollikut. The day after Ollikut's death, and only 40 miles (64 km) from the Canadian border, Chief Joseph called a halt to what has become known as the Nez Perce War.

Chief Joseph's words of surrender are famous. We have no way of knowing if these were his exact words. They were translated from Sahaptin into English, and they were written down by a newspaperman who may have made some changes for the sake of clarity or impact. That really doesn't matter. Whatever the differences in words might be, the despair and pain that gave meaning to his words remains clear:

Tell General Howard I know his heart. What he told me before, I have in my heart. I am tired of fighting. Our chiefs are killed. Looking Glass is dead. Toohoolhoolzote is dead. The old men are all dead. It is the young men who say yes and no. He who led on the young men is dead. It is cold and we have no blankets. The little children are freezing to death. My people, some of them, have run away to the hills and have no blankets, no food; not one knows where they are — perhaps freezing to death. I want to have time to look for my children and see how many I can find. Maybe I shall find them among the dead.

Hear me, my chiefs. I am tired; my heart is sick and sad. From where the sun now stands I will fight no more forever.

The soldiers had a grudging respect for the Nez Perce who had fought almost to victory against great odds. They shepherded them home with care. And at each little settlement along the way, whites came out of their homes with food and clothing for the tattered band. It was easy to be charitable now that the Nez Perce had lost everything. Joseph and the others were sent to a number of other reservations aboard crowded flatboats, trains, and wagons, and by foot. Eventually, those who lived through it all returned home, but Joseph did not. He became a celebrity, went to Wahington, D.C., to speak for his people, but was never allowed to live on the Nez Perce reservation. He was permitted to visit his father's grave and was touched that the whites had carefully tended it.

Today, the Nez Perce number a little more than a thousand persons, their numbers depleted by inter-marriage and intermingling with other tribes. They have brought a number of lawsuits against the U.S. government for compensation for the lands they lost, and have been awarded several million dollars so far. Money does not make up for the injustices done the Nez Perce many generations ago, but what would?

The federal government has provided them with schools and medical care but little else. The Nez Perce, like many others, have few economic resources or opportunities on reservation land. They turned to crafts — they are noted for their corn-husk bags — and, more recently, to trying to attract tourists. Now they are looking to build gambling casinos to attract more visitors. Such casinos have proven successful on other Indian reservations where state restrictions on gambling do not apply. They bring their tribes a lot of money, even wealth, and while some people are opposed to gambling, it is natural that the Nez Perce might finally be able to tap into the kind of riches that others sought for so long in this great land that once belonged only to the Indians.

GLOSSARY

Bloodletting opening a vein to let out blood thought to have gone bad.

Breechclouts strips of skins suspended from a band around the waist to conceal and protect the midsection.

Camas blue-flowered plant growing from an onion-like bulb that the Nez Perce enjoyed eating.

Coups killing, injuring, or even touching an enemy in a raid.

Kouse a root eaten boiled or as dried cakes.

Reservations land set aside by the federal government for the sole use of American Indian nations.

Shamans healers and spiritual leaders.

Sinew tissue that connects muscle to bone.

Trachoma a contagious eye disease that causes irritation and granulation of the conjunctiva or moist lining of the eye and scarring of the cornea; it can lead to blindness.

FOR FURTHER READING

Avery, Susan, and Linda Skinner. *Extraordinary American Indians*. Chicago: Childrens Press, 1992.

Howes, Kathi. *The Nez Perce*. Vero Beach, Fla.: Rourke Publications, 1990.

Osinski, Alice. *The Nez Perce*. Chicago: Childrens Press, 1988.

Sneve, Virginia Driving Hawk. *The Nez Perce*. New York: Holiday House, 1994.

Trafzer, Clifford E. *The Nez Perce*. New York: Chelsea House, 1992.

INDEX

ABOUT THE AUTHOR

Madelyn Klein Anderson is a graduate of Hunter College, New York University, and Pratt Institute. She is a registered occupational therapist and has a master's degree in library science. She is a former Army officer and senior editor of books for young people at a major publishing house. At present she is a consultant in the Office of Educational Research at the Board of Education of the City of New York and is writing her fifteenth book.